KALEIDOSCOPE

THE SALEM WITCH TRIALS

by
Edward F. Dolan

BENCHMARK BOOKS

MARSHALL CAVENDISH
NEW YORK

Benchmark Books
Marshall Cavendish Corporation
99 White Plains Road
Tarrytown, NY 10591
Website: www.marshallcavendish.com

Library of Congress Cataloging-in-Publication Data
Dolan, Edward F., date
The Salem witch trials / by Edward F. Dolan.
   p.cm. – (Kaleidoscope)
Includes bibliographical references and index.
ISBN 0-7614-1302-2
1. Trials (Witchcraft)—Massachusetts—Salem—History—17th century—Juvenile literature. 2. Witchcraft—Massachusetts—
Salem—History—17th century—Juvenile literature. [1. Trials (Witchcraft)—Massachusetts—Salem. 2. Witchcraft—
Massachusetts—Salem—History.] I. Title. II. Kaleidoscope (Tarrytown, N.Y.)
KFM2478.8.W5 D65 2001   345.744'50288—cd21   00-049798

Photo research by Anne Burns Images

Cover Photo: Salem Witch Museum

The photographs in this book are used by permission and through the courtesy of: Granger Collection: 5, 9, 10, 13, 14, 17, 18, 21, 33. North Wind Pictures: 22, 25, 26, 34, 37, 38, 42. Massachusetts Historical Society: 6. Denvers ArchivalCenter: 29. Peabody Essex Institute: 30. Corbis Images: 41.

Printed in Italy

6 5 4 3 2 1

CONTENTS

STRANGE HAPPENINGS

The people of Salem Village were mystified in early 1692. Strange things were happening in their village. Stories were going around about two young girls who would throw themselves on the floor at home, roll around, and scream in pain. Sometimes, they would crawl on all fours and growl like animals.

The girls were Betty Parris and her cousin Abigail Williams. Betty was nine years old, and Abigail was eleven. Both lived with Betty's father—Reverend Samuel Parris, the village minister.

A terrified family would hold a child down and pray over her when she seemed to be the victim of witchcraft. This picture is from an engraving made in the 1800s.

6

UNDER THE POWER OF A WITCH?

Reverend Parris and the villagers were frightened by what was happening. Betty and Abigail seemed to be in the clutches of an evil spirit. Could it be a witch?

But did the people of Salem village in the Massachusetts Bay Colony really believe there were such things as witches? Indeed they did. The belief was part of their religious thinking as Puritans. They were certain that the Devil constantly tempted everyone to sin against God. Witches were creatures who did this awful work for Satan.

The Reverend Samuel Parris, Betty Parris's father.

Further, the villagers had come from Europe. There, the belief in witches had terrified people for centuries. Thousands of people had been hunted down and punished as witches. Their crime was considered so terrible that its punishment was death by burning or hanging.

This illustration is from a German woodcut of the 1500s. Witchcraft was considered such a terrible crime throughout Europe that it was punished by hanging or burning at the stake. The same punishments were brought to America by the early settlers.

The people of Salem—and other early American communities— were especially suspicious of old women who were physically ugly. Today, this is considered prejudice.

10

Witches were usually thought to be ugly old women, though younger women and a few men could be found among them. If Betty and Abigail were indeed bewitched, it was up to Reverend Parris to free them. There was only one way he could do so. He had to find which villager was harming them and then drive that person away.

But he had no idea who was doing the harm. Witches were evil on the inside. On the outside, even though said to be ugly, they looked like ordinary people. Only their victims knew who they were— and the girls refused to say.

The two shook their heads and remained silent when Reverend Parris first questioned them. But he went on asking, until they broke down and uttered three names: Sarah Good, Sarah Osborne, and Tituba Indian.

With these names, the stage was set for one of the strangest court trials in American history.

THE TWO SARAHS AND TITUBA

The names of Sarah Good and Sarah Osborne did not surprise the minister. Both women fit the picture of a witch that most people had in their minds. Both were known for their bad tempers. Sarah Good lived as a beggar, asking for handouts and cursing those who refused her. Sarah Osborne often quarreled with her neighbors.

A bad-tempered woman, as depicted here, might very well be accused of witchcraft.

14

But the name of Tituba horrified Parris. She was a slave who worked for his family. Betty and Abigail then confessed a terrible fact. For months, they and four friends had been meeting secretly with Tituba to hear her tell stories of her former home in the West Indies. Soon, the friends began to act as crazed as the two girls. Tituba must have bewitched them all!

Tituba tells stories of her childhood in the West Indies to the frightened Betty Parris and Abigail Williams and two of their young friends.

15

In March 1692, two judges came to Salem to question the three accused women. The judges were to decide whether they should be charged as witches and sent to trial.

The village meeting house was packed when the questioning began. In turn, Sarah Good and Sarah Osborne stepped before the judges. Both denied being witches. But then the judges had them face their two accusers. A single glance set Betty and Abigail to screaming in terror.

Cotton Mather was a well-known Massachusetts minister who wrote a book in favor of the Salem Witch Trials.

17

This convinced everyone that the girls were indeed under the spell of the Sarahs. The girls screamed again when Tituba faced them. But Tituba did not deny being a witch. She confessed to serving the Devil.

The judges ordered the Sarahs to stand trial. Tituba, however, was set free. This was because of an old belief that once people confessed to being witches, they were no longer dangerous. They had broken Satan's hold on them. (Many historians suspect that Tituba confessed because she knew it would keep her from being tried.)

Sarah Good and Sarah Osborne are pictured being questioned by the judges who will decide their fate.

THE FIRST TRIAL

The first of the Salem witch trials began three months later, on June 2. It did not actually take place in Salem village, but nearby in the larger town of Salem. (The village had been named after the town.)

Nor was it the two Sarahs who were brought to trial. Sarah Osborne had died some days earlier, and Sarah Good would not go to court until the end of June. The first person to be tried was Bridget Bishop, the owner of the local inn.

Cotton Mather wrote a booklet on witchcraft, the cover of which is pictured here. He worked forty-three years as a minister and wrote 450 books on many different topics.

The *Wonders* of the *Invisible World*:

Being an Account of the

TRYALS

OF

Several Witches,

Lately Excuted in

NEW-ENGLAND:

And of several remarkable Curiosities therein Occurring.

Together with,

I. Observations upon the Nature, the Number, and the Operations of the Devils.

II. A short Narrative of a late outrage committed by a knot of Witches in *Swede-Land*, very much resembling, and so far explaining, that under which *New-England* has laboured.

III. Some Councels directing a due Improvement of the Terrible things lately done by the unusual and amazing Range of *Evil-Spirits* in *New-England*.

IV. A brief Discourse upon those *Temptations* which are the more ordinary Devices of Satan.

By COTTON MATHER.

Published by the Special Command of his EXCELLENCY the Governcur of the Province of the *Massachusetts-Bay* in *New-England*.

Printed first, at *Boston* in *New-England*; and Reprinted at *London*, for *John Dunton*, at the *Raven* in the *Pudtery*. 1693.

Bridget was the first to face the court because of the strange happenings in Salem. The age-old fear of witches had electrified the villagers and set their imaginations to running wild. Many—especially the children—were accusing their neighbors of being witches. Bridget was among the accused.

Bridget Bishop, the owner of a Salem inn, was the first person to go on trial for witchcraft.

What is known today as mass hysteria was gripping little Salem. Hysteria means "intense fear," and it becomes mass hysteria when it grips a number of people at the same time.

Mass hysteria can be easily seen in the case of a villager named Martha Corey. After several girls accused her of being a witch, she was questioned by a panel of judges to see if she should stand trial. The girls watched, and whenever Corey folded her hands on her lap, they screamed that she was pinching their hands. As a result, she was placed in prison to await trial.

Several young women accused Martha Corey of witchcraft. As Martha was being questioned, the girls began to scream in terror.

Soon the hysteria was spreading beyond Salem village. People in neighboring towns began to see witches all around them. By June, one hundred people were in jail, awaiting trial.

The trial of Bridget Bishop, like those that followed, was conducted by a panel of judges. They questioned two men who had made repairs on her inn. The two men said that, while working, they had found several rag dolls with pins stuck in them.

The hysteria over witchcraft began to spread far and wide. In this illustration, a man named John Sevier is standing trial for witchcraft in distant North Carolina.

27

To the judges, this meant just one thing: black magic. It was an ancient practice that was especially popular in the West Indies and Africa. According to its beliefs, people could cause great pain in someone they hated by sticking pins in a doll made in the hated person's image. The discovery of the dolls in Bridget's inn was enough to convict her. She was hanged on June 10.

Bridget Bishop was among the unfortunates to be found guilty and hanged.

Black magic played only a small part in the trials, however. The greatest role of all was played by "spectral evidence."

What was spectral evidence? People believed that the victims of witches had a special power. They could see things that others could not see. These things were specters—the ghosts of the witches. For example: one woman, Mary Warren, had to stand trial because Abigail Williams swore she could see Mary's specter. Abigail claimed that the specter had once pinched her.

Spectral evidence played an important role in the witch trials. Here, Rebecca Nurse is declared innocent. But the judges soon changed their verdict when her young accusers claimed their lives were in jeopardy.

Because the victims were believed to have a special power, their word was accepted without argument. There was no way to prove that they were lying or imagining things.

One of the most dramatic cases of spectral evidence concerned a woman named Rebecca Nurse. When she was judged innocent, the girls who had accused her began screaming that her ghost was trying to kill them. The jurors then changed their verdict to guilty.

A punishment perhaps more cruel than hanging was used during the trials. It was inflicted on eighty-year-old Giles Corey, one of the few men accused of being a witch. He refused to enter a plea of either guilty or not guilty when told that he must stand trial. Under an old British law, he could not be tried until he did so.

Women were not the only ones who were accused of witchcraft. Eighty-year-old Giles Corey was accused and found guilty of witchcraft. He met his death in one of the cruelest ways imaginable.

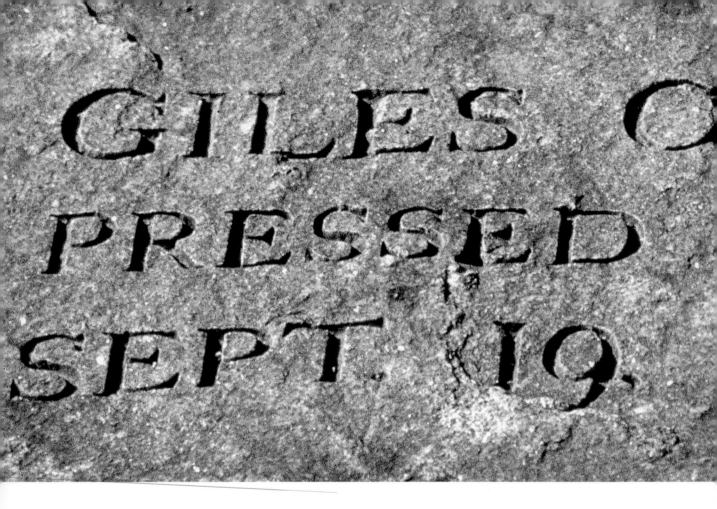

GILES C
PRESSED
SEPT 19.

It permitted him to be tortured into changing his mind. The old man was placed on his back beneath a board. Then heavy rocks were piled on the board, slowly crushing him. The torture would stop only if he agreed to enter a plea.

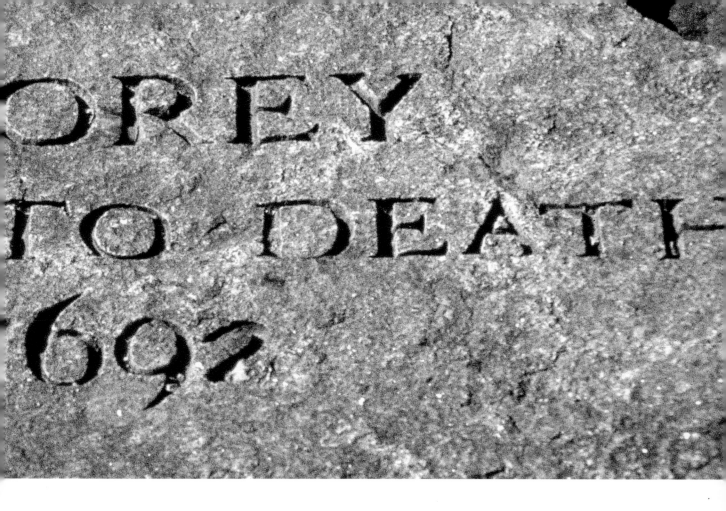

Corey stubbornly held his tongue. He died when his rib cage collapsed.

This memorial stone was placed at Salem in honor of Giles Corey.

A SUMMER OF TRIALS

The trials continued throughout the summer. During that time, some four hundred people were accused of being witches. Of their number, two hundred were in jail and awaiting trial.

Several people were tried at a time. By late summer, twenty of the accused were dead. Only those who denied being witches lost their lives. All others, like Tituba, were freed.

The hysteria that gripped Massachusetts began to fade in the fall. More and more, the accusers were looking like either fools or liars. They were running out of people to name and had taken to accusing the colony's most respected citizens.

Another man found guilty of witchcraft—the Reverend Burroughs—kneels in prayer just seconds before his death by hanging.

In October, the governor of Massachusetts put an end to the trials. He was disgusted with them. His disgust was shared by a growing number of people.

There were several reasons for the citizens' changing feelings. First, they recognized that most of the accusers were young girls who liked drawing attention to themselves. Second, they realized that the girls, as Puritans, lived by strict rules of proper behavior and were given scant time to enjoy themselves.

A young girl accuses a soldier, Captain Alden, of being a witch.

Third, Salem village stood on the edge of a wilderness that was made frightening by unfriendly Indians. In total, then, the trials broke the monotony of life for the girls and, at the same time, provided them with a means for temporarily forgetting their fears.

There was also a growing dislike of the spectral evidence allowed in the trials. As time passed, it struck an increasing number of people as unjust because there was no way of proving it wrong.

A Salem family barricade their home against an Indian attack. The fear of such attacks may have been one of the causes of the witchcraft hysteria. The drama of the trials took people's minds off such fears.

Many of the accused were yet to go to court when the trials were cancelled. Most were acquitted in December hearings. The rest were then pardoned by the governor.

One of the judges apologizes for his part in the trials and asks to be forgiven.

By year's end, one of the strangest courtroom dramas in American history was over. It was a terrible episode. However, eventually these trials had a healthy effect on the country. Massachusetts set aside a day of public mourning for those who had been executed. Judges and jurors asked to be forgiven for their verdicts. And, most important of all, spectral evidence was never again permitted in trials. American law had taken a major step away from superstition.

TIMELINE

Early 1692

Betty Parris and Abigail Williams begin to behave oddly. They name Sarah Good, Sarah Osborne, and Tituba Indian as witches.

March 1692

Two judges come to Salem Village. Tituba is released but the two Sarahs are ordered to stand trial.

June 1692

One hundred people are in jail and awaiting trial on charges of witchcraft. Bridget Bishop is found guilty and is hanged.

Summer 1692

Giles Corey is crushed to death.

Autumn 1692

Four hundred people are now accused of being witches, with two hundred locked in jail while awaiting trial. Twenty have been hanged.

October 1692

The governor of Massachusetts puts an end to the trials.

December 1692

All remaining prisoners awaiting trial are acquitted. The rest are pardoned.

FIND OUT MORE

BOOKS:

Cavendish, Richard, Editor. *Man, Myth and Magic: And Illustrated Encyclopedia of the Supernatural* (vol. 18). New York: Marshall Cavendish Corporation, 1970.

Hill, Douglas. *Witches and Magic-Makers.* New York: Alfred A. Knopf, 1997.

Rice, Earle. *The Salem Witch Trials.* San Diego, CA: Lucent Books, 1997.

Roach, Marilynne K. *In the Days of the Salem Witch Trials.* Boston: Houghton Mifflin, 1996.

Van Der Linde, Laurel. *The Devil in Salem Village: The Story of the Salem Witchcraft Trials.* Brookfield, CT: Millbrook Press, 1992.

Wilson, Lori Lee. *The Salem Witch Trials.* Minneapolis, MN: Lerner Publications, 1997.

WEBSITES:

Salem@nationalgeographic.com
http:///www.nationalgeographic.com/features/97/splashx.html

The Salem Witch Museum
http://www.salemwitchmuseum.com

Salem Witch Trial Chronology
http://www.salemweb.com/memorial/default.htm

AUTHOR'S BIO

Edward F. Dolan is the author of over one hundred nonfiction books for young people and adults. He has written on medicine and science, law, history, folklore, and current social issues. Mr. Dolan is a native Californian, born in the San Francisco region and raised in Southern California. In addition to writing books, he has been a newspaper reporter and a magazine editor. He currently lives in the northern part of the state.

INDEX

Page numbers for illustrations are in boldface.